Copyright © Ma
First printing ed

All rights reserved. No part of this publication may be reproduced, distributed, or transmitted in any form or by any means, including photocopying, recording, or other electronic or mechanical methods, without the prior written permission of the publisher, except in the case of brief quotations embodied in critical reviews and certain other noncommercial uses permitted by copyright law.

While all attempts have been made to verify the information provided in this publication, neither the author nor the publisher assumes any responsibility for errors, omissions, or contrary interpretations of the subject matter herein. Adherence to all applicable laws and regulations, including international, federal, state, and local governing professional licensing, business practices, advertising, and all other aspects of doing business in the US, Canada, or any other jurisdiction is the sole responsibility of the purchaser or reader.

Any perceived slight of any individual or organization is purely unintentional.

The information and advice contained in this book are intended as a voluntary general guide. This book should not be relied on as medical advice. Neither the author nor the publisher are responsible for diagnosing or treating any health needs. This book is not intended to be medical advice. A qualified medical professional should be contacted if you have any health problems or underlying health problems. Furthermore, the author does not personally know any reader and refers to readers as "friend" in fiction.

Table of Contents

Chapter 1 – DENIAL	Page 1

Chapter 2 – ANGER	Page 39

Chapter 3 – BARGAINING	Page 88

Chapter 4 – DEPRESSION	Page 112

Chapter 5 – ACCEPTANCE	Page 151

Dedication page

Follow the path you originally had in your head and don't deviate from it. Everything around you will continue to crumble until then. This is *your* calling, finish the book.

Dedicated to:
London Bell
My Triplets
Those with a voice too subtle to be heard
Those simply at a loss for words
Those on the outside looking in, wanting to begin to understand

Dear reader, we are now friends. Hi friend.

Grief
Is A Five
Letter
Word

Thought 1

Brace yourself.
If nobody else did, I'll be the first to say— it did happen.
No, unfortunately it was not a bad dream.
Breathe, allow yourself room and grace to grasp reality.

Thought 68

I took the first sip of grief, and it was as bitter as my father's mistress; reality flavored brew.

Denial

I'm fine. There's nothing wrong with me. At least nothing enough to need therapy. And if something did bother me, I have the power to block it out. And if there's something bothering me, it must be something bothering everybody. Because *"I'm fine."* and *"It's fine."* are the only responses given to *"How are you?"* and *"How's your day?"*

The ratio is off. I know everyone can't be okay on every and any given day. Look, I'm not trying to divert the focus off of me and on to you, so let me just address it today. I'm fine but when I say that, know that on a good day, I'm fine only ever goes skin deep. Mentally and emotionally, I can't even begin to speak. I got nothing.

Thought 12

The younger you is cheering for you if no one else is. Growth is not a straight line, it's a curly one.

Butterfly Effect

Movement,
In the slightest form will shift your life.
Turning left instead of right.
Turning right instead of left.
You ought to bid on you, you're worth your highest bet.
What else could you lose; you've already lost your mind.
Do you want it back?
Take it.
Go give life a try, one more time.
And not a half-ass try.
Try like you mean it this time.
You might find something that's actually worth the find.
Small, unsure, and clumsy movement is still movement.
One foot forward, one stumble at a time.
Do it for you.
Beautifully unpredicted, unscripted.
That straight line you drew, twist it.
That cup that's filled to the brim, tip it.
Let's move.

Thought 3

They are only calling you to try and gauge if you're ahead or behind them.

Frenemy

You despise me yet admire me.
I inspire yet erupt the lava in you.
So tell me, when did envy turn you into an enemy?
Or have you been an enemy disguised all along?
You were never meant to be digested.
But since you were, I've caught on to you.
We were friends because I loved you;
yet enemies because at your core, you've always hated me.

Thought 15

A friendship you're only hanging on to because the length of time you've known each other is not a friendship at all.

Thought 82

What you see in front of you is the real authentic them, at least in this present time. Who they were is no longer and who they could be is not reality. You do not have the power to change anyone. Only they can do the work needed for change and that's if they even want to.
Gracefully step out of their way and continue your healing journey.

Place Holder

He said I'm strong and he's seen me do it before.
What's wrong with carrying the weight of the world a little while more?
And yes, I already told him to leave.
I already told him to get up, get out, take his things, and leave my key.
He only did the first three.
Then he came back while I was asleep.
He came back even more comfortable and confident than before.
How could I tell?
Because he doesn't even snore, but that night he started to snore.
I could be somewhere meeting my husband and receiving so much more, if only I would close this door.
Plus, I overheard him pre-planning his own life.
Whispering on the phone to a woman whose number is saved as: My *Future Wife*.

Thought 47

You are what you say. You are what you write down. Never underestimate the power of the tongue, hand, and the black ink pen.

The Power Of The Pen

I am worthy.
I am enough.
I am deserving of a life that's not tough.
I am growing.
I am healing.
I am human and I have feelings.
I have meaning.
I have a purpose.
I won't stop until I am done.
I am wide awake.
I am winding down.
I am giving myself some slack.
I am going at my own pace.
I am allowed a break.
I am recharging then I will be back.
I am beautiful.
I am full.
I am whole even with a hole in my heart.
I am going don't you rush me.
I am allowed to stop, reset, and restart.
I am wanted.
I am needed, even if not by you.
I am strong.
I am equipped.
Everything I give power to will come true.

Smile

You have to do better than hold it all together, you have to smile while doing it too.
Grace me and stroke my ego until I say you can be through.
Give people something easy to see.
Smile, quit making it harder than it has to be.
The smile is for us, if it's real, forced, or fake
doesn't really matter.
Just smile for now, you can frown right after.
We just want the laughter.
Cry on the inside.
Don't let your raw, real emotions seep through.
We don't want to be able to see what you've been through.
Not even for a minute.
We'd rather ignore your grief all together, than stand with you in it.

Thought 50

"Smile it can't be that bad."

Signed,
A person who is oblivious that it can be and is indeed that bad; but to the tenth power.

I know it's more convenient and appealing if they'd just smile but be selfless for once and hear me out. People are allowed to feel and frown. You might have caught them during the one time they took their smiling mask off, let their cheeks relax, and let their guard down. They don't owe you a smile. Give them something to smile about rather than a command followed by a critique and hope that gesture makes them smile. If it doesn't, that is perfectly okay too.
I'm protective of my friend; this one specifically. Please mind your own face and business.

GPS

Has anyone seen this girl?
She could be across the world by now.
She's usually always laughing or
on her way somewhere to eat.
She's always dancing, wandering, moving her feet.
That girl never stays in one place for long.
She goes ahead anyway and sings the song.
Although she probably shouldn't try to sing along.
Her hair is long, well longer than mines.
It's the same length mine would be if I hadn't cut it
for the third time.
I'll do whatever it takes to find her.
I mean, how hard could it be?
To GPS a route back to me.
I hope you find yourself too.
Do whatever you have to do, to reunite with you.

Thought 8

You aren't able to find or feel like yourself after a life-changing event because you're looking for a version of you that does not exist anymore. You must get acquainted with the stranger in the mirror. They are just as captivating. Get to know that new person, the new you is worth knowing. Finding yourself is realizing you are not lost; you're right in front of you. Waiting to be recognized and reintroduced to you, by you.

Thought 17

You have to acknowledge the pain, the giant amongst us in this teeny-tiny room, to begin to move past it.

You Forgot Something

Your mistress told you and I that I would take up too much space.
And you let her be right, you didn't even put up a fight.
You started a whole new life with your new wife
and you took everything with you, even my house key.
But you forgot me.
Every man you slept with turned into your new husband
and now you're moving to another city again.
Am I invisible?
Because you grabbed all the things you need, but you always seem to leave me.
Work turns you every which way but loose, so I hardly see you.
But you put your own neck in a noose.
Because I have a good memory and I remember you.
You said, "I work so much because I want to, not have to."
I heard you tell Ms. Kline nine years ago that work was your baby, and I couldn't help but wonder what that made me.
For your addiction you'll stay up telling stories to strangers all night.
I saw that, I see it all.
I've seen you lie, cheat, and steal steel for a refill.
I've seen you change from professional to strung out and back to professional again before the weekend ends; to juggle your relationship with drugs.

GRIEF IS A FIVE LETTER WORD

The love you'd get from me doesn't require any of the above.
I can love you safer than a drug.
To that you said I wouldn't understand because drugs love you better than love.
That doesn't even make sense, but by the sound of it I can't compete.
Look, I'm not trying to make you late, I know you have things to do and places to be.
I just thought you should know; you forgot something.

Thought 29

You were designed specifically for your life and the events that happen in it. Good and bad, they were meant for you to endure. I wish we could all just eat the good and simply pick out all the bad. It just doesn't work like that.

Thought 69

Procrastination is my body's trauma response to fear and expected disappointment. I savor the taste of Tuesday while sacrificing and sabotaging Wednesday.

Dead Rose Stems

Let go, before you turn your hand raw from holding on so tight.
All that's left is a thought, and that's even wrong.
You keep bending reality though, so it just seems right.

Thought 89

If you ever feel someone is lucky or you find yourself envying their life, just remember, every person has their own book of pain and a pitcher full of tears they've had to cry.

What Makes You Sleep Better At Night

Some things are that good.
You've convinced yourself that everyone is pretending.
So, nobody gets a happy ending?
A life that appears to be good must be fake, is what you tell yourself to cope.
But what if it really is as pretty as it's wrote?
What if there is no other side to the pictures they post?
I think that's what would hurt the most, because you've been waiting for your turn.
But they have too.
Behind the scenes everyone isn't lying or hiding the ugly truth.
Be positive, try to focus on what that looks like for you.
Growth is realizing you're subconsciously hoping for bad in someone else's life, just so that you can sleep a little better at night.

Thought 81

You do need help. We all do. Maybe not in that area, but in this one or that other one. The help you need might be in an area you refuse to acknowledge even exists. I am the friend that will tell you what you need to hear because you have no choice but to grow around me.

Neck Tattoos And Clay Vases

Grief is not a sickness like a cold to get over.
Grief is something that you wear, it will stay with you forever.
This is a mandatory tattoo that no one is exempt from going through.
You'll jump from stage to stage in no particular pattern or form.
Regardless of the order, allow yourself permission to acknowledge each season.
Some days, you'll smile and complete a million tasks while your hair hangs low, so that others don't know you have a neck tattoo.
Another day, you'll forget good days randomly do exist and you'll pull your hair high into the bun you used to wear.
That is, until someone points at the ink and yells *"Smile, your grief is showing."*
Thanks for reminding me to put my hair down and fake smile.
Even if you numb the area and get the tattoo removed, a scar will appear as a stand in for the missing ink.
Tempting each passerby to ask, *"How'd you get that scar?"*
Grief is yours to keep, to have, and to hold.
A lifelong pottery class, with a grief shaped vase to mold.

Thought 72

Running from reality will only make you too tired to face it once it catches up to you.

Smoke Signal

Self, are you ok?
I'm asking because no one else did today.
It's not their job to anyway, but that's beside the point.
Are we exercising?
Sleeping through the night?
Still wandering?
This time did we choose left or right?
Tell me we're still traveling the world.
Crossing cities off our list.
Still taking road trips.
Still collecting magnets.
Do we still pump our gas on pump three?
Do you still think about those three?
I don't care how much money we have
or if we're married or single.
If we are ok, just let off a pretty pink smoke signal.

If we're not, send black.

Thought 16

You'll only ever see what your mind is ready to see. While in denial, reality will always feel offensive.

Parasite

Some people will use you until you have nothing left to give.
Next, they'll act like for them, nothing is all you ever did.
And then?

There is no then.
Hostess, you are nothing to them.
To them, a host is all you've ever been.

Thought 93

Denial meets reality at the fork in the road. You'll move forward once you let reality drive the rest of the way.

Thought 9

What if I just skipped town, changed my name and number, and vanished into thin air? Home was always wherever you were at. You told me I could always come back home if I needed to. Now that you're gone, there's no such place called home.

Mornings At The Car Shop

I travel for survival, although it used to be just for fun.
Luck is on my side because the people I run into aren't half bad.
I can be having the time of my life, and I'll still feel a small piece of sad.
I want to share these memories with people I do more with than just cross paths.
I think they're starting to sense that I'm out here all alone.
Why else would somebody be walking up the side of the road?
To another shop named another name I don't really care to know.
Writing and waiting, so that I can go anywhere in the world other than what's supposed to be home.

Thought 55

Trying to balance working to survive and watering my passion to stay alive. What a sad yet beautifully strategic act to watch at the circus I call my life.

Mistress

Writing is my mistress; she feeds and waters my soul.
Her words protectively wrap around me like warmth on a cold winter night; something my job would never do.
She wrote her name across my brain in smooth, black, velvety ink.
If I could spend every day with her I would.

Thought 76

Find your passion and let it pull you towards healing. The two of you were meant to spend your life together.

Am I Adopted?

This cold life couldn't biologically be my own.
I'm grown, I deserve to know.
Go ahead and tell me now, I promise I won't get mad.
Is that really my dad?
Are you really my mom?
I won't stop asking until you say the right answer.
The answer is supposed to be no.
If I'm not supposed to be here, please let me go.
If you were just going to hurt me, you could've given me away.
And I already know what you're going to say.
I get it, I heard you before, I was planned.
But you didn't plan to get bold and blunt me specifically.
You told me before.
I'd rather roll the dice and be sat at a random door, or accidentally left at a convenience store; for a second chance at parents that liked me more.
Ones that won't leave my heart so bruised and sore.

Thought 34

Practice mercy. The same mercy you'd want. Your mom, dad, grandparents, siblings, and friends have never been right here or right now. They might make a mistake you'd never make but remember, they aren't you. Consider all the trauma and grief they may have that could have shaped the way they think and process things.

This does not excuse them, it's still their job to unlearn toxic behavior. Forgiving is not a re-entry ticket. You don't owe anyone a second, third, and fourth chance to hurt you. Have mercy for you, so you can gain closure and understanding.

Thought 25

You did the best you could with the hand you were dealt.

Anger

I'm mad, and I have every right to be. I am allowed to embrace this emotion and its ugly entirety. I see red. My ears, fuming and hot to the touch. I know my face is showing it, you don't have to tell me. I have no desire to smile so I can appear more appealing to you. You don't have any idea what I've just been through. I'm mad. And no, I'm not telling you what's wrong because there's nothing you can say or do. Plus, I didn't ask you to; so I don't even want to see or hear you attempt to. The wrath of my emotions are capable of leaving deep scars time won't even heal if I allow anger to stampede through at its own pace and leisure.

I refuse to use anyone as a human punching bag. I am selfless enough to understand nobody is obligated to be around me as I conquer this stage. I am conscious enough to realize my negative energy must be transferred to a positive outlet because although I am giving it permission to visit, anger has no house key in me. I am left engulfed in rage; I've been swallowed whole by fury, but I refuse to be digested by it. I. Am. Mad. This anger is strong enough to destroy everything around me that's left standing, yet fragile enough to break into tiny shards of aching tears.

Thought 44

Some people want you to stay angry. Your rage brings them joy and entertainment. Disappoint them with your growth. Bore them by healing and seeking out happiness.

Ballpoint Pen

I've always chosen pen over pencil, because I meant what I said.
I've always chosen pen over pencil, even when I probably should've chosen pencil instead.
I've always just taken the risk and wrote with a black ballpoint pen.
If it's wrong, I'll put a single line through and rewrite it then.
Velvety, black, bold, and permanent.
I'd choose it over, and over, and over again.

Thought 77

The words they tried to silence are sautéed, heavily seasoned with soul, and served in a deep dish. A dish with such depth, you have no choice but to taste every word and all its flavors; or choke on them. You choose. Either way, you will hear me roar.

Thought 24

They want me to support and root for them, but where were they with my bouquet of support tied with a big bow made out of roots? The room grew silent when it was time to do the same for me.

Owl Eyes

Everything is noted.
Perched quietly, I observe.
Every criss you cross, I see.
Unnoticed from below, but I sit in the tallest of tall trees.
Watching how you treat others versus me.
My eyes, like doors left ajar, show off a small but bright light.
You've realized I've been watching you, but you don't know how long.
Frozen in uncertainty, you stand behind me yet face to face.
My eyes, strikingly round like saucer plates,
If I blink, they might just break.
You want to run, like always.
You stare admiringly yet intimidated by my face, talons, and feathers.
Such a strong, pretty, pretty bird.
How much have you heard?
How much have you seen?
How much do you know?
I guess you'll never know.
You're plagued with the uncertainty birthed from your own doings.
I spread my wings as you brace yourself—

Thought 90

You are the dish at the family function that I do like. The tasty bites I don't have to spit out when our parents aren't looking. I grieve the loss of life being simple enough for us to be at the same place at the same time.

Thought 28

There was no way to stop that from happening. You know exactly what thing I'm talking about. Yes, that one. Even if you went back and did things differently. It was written in stone to happen exactly like that before you were even born.
The what-ifs that you replay in your head will taunt you and even kill you if you let them. Stop that.

GRIEF IS A FIVE LETTER WORD

Until Next Time

I kick myself every time you cross my mind because you left, and I didn't get to say goodbye.
I was on my way, I only missed you by a moment.
The last thing I'd ever want is for you to think I didn't care.
Understand that it would've ached so much more to die while you were standing there.

You're gone and now the last conversation we will ever have is one that left off bad.
I'm angry.
I'm mad, I'm mad that I can't tell you I'm sorry or that I take everything I said back.
I get it, but look at the other side.
You'll never end another night in a fight.
You'll communicate and try and make it right.
You'll hold loved ones even more tight.
And if that conversation had to go bad so that better ones could be had, I'll gladly take that.
I know you're mad, but release that, I'm not mad.

Everything happened so fast.
One second you were here and the next you were gone.
I didn't even get the chance to say goodbye.
You couldn't have ever controlled that, and this is not a goodbye, it's until next time.

Thought 95

It doesn't matter how much someone else wants it for you, you have to want better for yourself. The rest will fall into place.

Addiction

Selling sweet dreams to get whatever they want.
Passing out lies to friends and family so they'll shut up.
I didn't come to sugar coat.
I'm exhausted, I've heard enough.
You can beg, cry, ask when, and why.
They won't change until they escape what has a grip on them.
And who's to say they even want to be freed?
They've been blinded, but who said they even want to see?
Imagining the colorful life they could have if they'd just quit is only breaking your own spirit.
Quitting is as hard as they said.
You keep ignoring the signs that read danger in uppercase, bold font, and red.
The water is deep, cold, and unknown.
You swim out to them, in attempt to bring them back home.
Meanwhile for their addiction, they'll sell your arms and legs to the highest bidder.
Now both of you are in high water.
Their head afloat, as they use yours as a floatie.
The weight of them too much for *one* person to hold.
Bystanders silently gather around watching as your body sinks further down.
The two of you swapped spots, are you truly surprised that you've drowned?

Thought 23

I mourn the lifelong friendships I thought I gained when I hastily handpicked poison out of desperation; In attempt to be accepted and heard by someone, anyone.

Irreconcilable Differences

Ex friend, I'll say it again.
I'm stepping down from this high pedestal.
Down to a safer place.
One where if you push me a fourth time,
I won't fall and break my face.
And what was that you said?
Do you have to come too?
Yes, you do.
It's not optional and I've already packed for you.
This is the part where your phone dies.
You'll call back but you always subject switch.
I'm not in a laughing mood,
I don't feel like laughing with you.
You said I've been a good friend,
why is it so hard to follow suit?
I can help, what do you need me to do?
You won't even help me help you.
Actually, you know what, I'm sorry.
I should've taken the hints; I shouldn't have imposed.
The truth is I expect me from others and it's clicking now that it's been wrote.
I was wanting you to be a friend that's more like me and less like you.
You act the same exact way you said all the women in your family do.

The type of friend you are was inherited; it's been passed down to you.

Thought 18

Either they heard you and they just don't care, or they heard you and they don't have the thinking capacity to even begin to understand the severity of what they've done. Either way they heard you. Neither way is yours to try and over explain or fix.

Thought 56

I address everything that hurts no matter how small, because the child in me was silenced for so long. I am not overly sensitive I am emotionally aware and recognize what doesn't feel good. I will not allow you to penalize me for prioritizing ME and how I feel. I'll leave, I'll be wherever there is no penalty for choosing ME.

It Isn't That Deep

Don't call my accomplishments, dreams, and things little when you speak to me.
I noticed you only invited them to the fun but call me first to help you get something serious done.
I watched you clap and scream for him,
yet you conveniently lose your voice every time I win.
I'm not thinking too deep, I've caught on to you.
Deflecting and flipping it on me for reacting is just like you to do; instead of sitting in the truth.
Yes, it is, indeed that deep.
It's as deep as I perceive it to be.
That puddle may only wet the bottoms of your feet.
But to me, that same puddle is chin deep.
If I did the same to you, you'd sink.
You'd quickly and clearly point out exactly how it's deep.
But since it's just me, my feelings can go drown for all you care, while you peacefully sleep.
Today forward I choose to speak.
You don't get to decide what I should think.
Regarding me, it will always be that deep.

Thought 37

I'm sorry, they're never going to come say sorry because they're simply not sorry. They don't feel they did anything wrong. Don't try to force them to see the obvious. You will drive yourself insane trying to get them to see the pain they caused you while they peacefully sleep.

I'm Sorry

I bet you'd prefer if I allowed myself to be unheard.
Unable to put my emotions into words.
It would be best for you if I were confused.
Compelled to blame myself for the things that you do.
Why does my intellect intimidate you?
Does my confidence remind you of how much self-work you have yet to do?
I'm sorry, I won't let you blame me for how you act.
Me being emotionally aware should not make you feel attacked.
And why not take responsibility for your actions,
to showcase an example of empathy and compassion?
Since I'm so aware, right?
Wrong again, I'm sorry.
I bet you'd beam if I desperately took your accountability and said sorry to you for the things you say.
The emotional and mental drain you'd cost is too high of an expense to pay.
It would be a dishonor to my growth, if in your presence I stayed.

Thought 70

Time passed is not an apology. And no, you don't have to just get over it. If they feel like that, they can *just* stay away from you.

Thought 67

Pain births anger. Without pain, anger would not exist.

The Oldest Child

I always wanted an older sibling, so I could have some type
of life map with little notated warnings scribbled on the
back.
I want to lay my head on someone's shoulder so bad.
I want to deep sigh and cry.
I'm drained, I don't want to be first in line to bang and
bump my head.
But if not me, than who?
Someone has to.
Those second and third have the luxury of watching.
Watching wrong turns, stops and watching me reverse.
Laughing because nobody's older to teach me first,
so every step I take is cautious and rehearsed.
Meanwhile their hands are out, expecting me to
still splurge and pay.
All while fist fighting battles on their behalf,
for the reckless things they do and say.
I'm 21, there are strands of my hair that are grey.
They don't hear the tired in my voice.
They're blind to the wear and tear on my face.
And to them, I should have everything perfectly in place.
But in one and two years once they reached my age,
I asked for the same things they did, and they wanted
sympathy and grace.

Thought 36

Anger left unaddressed will run rampant like a wildfire destroying everything in its path.

Hurt People

I don't even like you.
I just wanted company.
In me, you really believed you had all you'd need.
You spoke so confidently about this wedding ring thing.
And just look at me— jealous of how you love me.
Jealous of how you do it so pure and openly.
Envious of how you assume you're entitled to a happy ending so effortlessly, especially with me.
I'll ball up that fairytale ending any chance I get.
You worthy?
I can't let you feel that.
Life's only been a pain for me.
I still have things to do for me.
You expect me to just toss you a happy ending?
I had to work hard and strive and strain for me.
And look, you're bleeding your hurt all over my good fur rug.
Let yourself out and do it fast, before you let in any bugs.

Thought 10

I break my own heart expecting pure love in a world full of envy and hate.

Lover Boy

Don't stop loving.
Don't let this emotionless world turn you cruel.
They can't even receive your love, to them it tastes like poison.
Or maybe love to them, is just a feeling that feels too foreign.
And that's their loss, it's not your fault.
It's not yours to have to heal.
Love openly and loudly, just be mindful of who you pass that warmth out to.
Some have a heart so cold; they will freeze yours for the satisfaction of seeing you frost bitten like them.
Lover boy, let love win.
Dust yourself off and love again.

Who Is This

This lady that's sitting beside me, I don't recognize her at all.
The one I knew looks nothing like you.
She doesn't have my mother's posture and she's not her weight.
She was a night owl like me, this lady doesn't even stay up late.
My mother would've sat on the phone with me for hours.
This lady here hardly talks.
My mother used to work just fine.
She took the medicine she was prescribed, and the medicine turned around and took her mind.
This lady here is content, but my mother, she wanted answers.
That medication was wrong, it gave me you and it kept her.

1, 2 My 3

Triplets.
Mother's intuition told me that you were going to leave.
I've heard that death comes in threes, that terrified me.
Yesterday I drove to the doctor to check on you, I have the pictures to prove.
She's 21, it's her first pregnancy, she'll be worrying until she's due.
I was told the three of you were okay, but I knew my effort would be in vain.
So I did what I always do, write.
I wrote for my life.
I wrote scared, alone and teary-eyed.
I wrote asking you three to fight for your lives.
I wrote for 13 minutes but it felt like all night.
Then I read my letter out loud three times.
I held my breath and went to sleep.
This poem, this one here, is to my three.
I've never heard a silence so loud or stood in a sorrow so deep.

7.12.16

Thought 22

I refuse to let grief cripple and rob me of a flourishing, abundant life.

Blood On My Sheets

It's an honor to be offered the most precious job of all.
But to be abruptly fired before my first day makes me feel so small and like it must be my fault.
All the seemingly reassuring comments feel like lemon and salt.
They feel like being vegan and force-fed meat.
When I'm discharged, I'll fill my baby shower bottles with tears so I can have something left to keep.

Thought 96

Saying you can't imagine my pain or that you could never be in my shoes is not the compliment or honor that you think it is. Trust me, silence tastes a lot better than those phrases. Stop trying to find the perfect words to say. There aren't any. Just stand with me. Just listen to hear my cry. Sometimes, a moment of silence is enough of a reply.

A Slice Of My Heart

So, how exactly do I resume my life?
I'll never be alright I lost a slice of my heart.
The flower I grew.
The purest love I knew.
 I wouldn't wish this on anyone.
To outlive your child.
To identify their face.
To witness the last breath that they take.
How am I supposed to resume my life?
They'd want me to fight.
Honor the things that they liked.
Not to resume, but reset, reconfigure, and redesign my life.
To sleep good at night.
To one day, be more than alright.

Thought 21

They wouldn't want you to be stagnant and sad. If they had a chance to come sit beside you, they'd probably use it to make you laugh.

Thought 92

It's easy to say what you would and wouldn't do, until it's you. Until you're in that exact predicament with the exact same experiences and mindset as the person who endured it, you can't definitively say. Don't just take the predicament and say what you would do. First, take on everything that person has mentally and physically up to that point, for the exact same duration, at their exact same age; then say what you'd do.

If I Were You

If you were me?
You can't tell me what you'd do while using those feet.
While using those thoughts and experiences that belong to you.
You can't just waltz across the finish line in my shoes.
You have to run the entire race.
Poor thing, you don't get time to tie, in my shoes.
Leave them unlaced.
Suffer, get pushed, fall and start to crawl at my pace my exact same way.
Then, tell me what you would do.
If you were me, you'd have the exact same scars and traumas.
You'd be threatened and groomed.
You'd have the exact same bruise.
You'd be identically mentally abused and used.
Give me back my damn shoes.
If you were me, you'd do what I did and choose what I choose.

Thought 48

If that one particular person was around, certain people wouldn't dare do the things they do or say. That person would stop as much bad from happening on their watch as they could, if given the chance. They weren't at that place at that time to protect you because they would without hesitation, naturally interfere with what your life was assigned to endure. Time would've never aligned for this *what if*. Everything had to happen this way. It's your job to figure out how to effectively share the lessons learned through life and the messages made from scratch out of pain.

Wait, I Can't Reach My Shield

If you were free, you would've protected me.
But you've fallen deep through the sidewalk's widest crack.
If only I could reach you, I know you'd have my back.
I deep sighed and out of frustration I did cry because I just want my shield back.
I tried to hide my hand like you said to do, but my all alone is showing.
These people know I'm unarmed.
They keep saying and doing what they know they wouldn't do if I had you.
I reached my arm deep into the depths of that crack.
I was determined to get you back.
My ear always rested on the roughest part of the cement.
I could hear the rowdiness of the other shields that went.
Even shoulder deep, l still couldn't reach.
And I still can't, no matter how much I've grown.
I have no choice but to wait until the sidewalk releases you on its own; and that day may or may not ever come around.
Listen, my shield is wedged between the crack in the ground so can you please stop aiming at me?
Of course, they still have no remorse.
In fact, I'm sure they're aiming at me more.
For being a warrior in a battlefield.
But mostly, for being a warrior that has no shield.

Thought 5

You helped rough up my story, now you're surprised I'm rowdy?

Thought 26

You weren't passed down any tools to survive yet you found a way. Don't let anyone tell you that's not impressive.

I Sewed My Wings Back On

Look what I did.
Why thank you, I had no choice but to.
They tore my wings off and threw them way over there.
They laughed at my disadvantage.
They teased and taunted me for the torture they inflicted.
Watching, hoping for me to be a statistic.
They tore my wings off and threw them way across a busy, rainy road.
They left me in the cold with nothing to wear but a tiny sweater made out of itchy, wild wool.
They left me for dead, with no tools.
I couldn't fly so I started to walk across the street.
I was ran over, dirty and wet.
I could no longer walk so I crawled, because I'm still worth my highest bet.
They tore my wings off and threw them where they thought I couldn't go.
They tore my wings off, so I taught myself how to sew.
They envy my strength.
Pride won't let them admit that was impressive.
Warm and dry, yet boiling with rage, taunting me this time for squeezing lemons into pink lemonade.
For making a way, when audacity was all that was left.
Deemed as bitter for speaking out about the bad things.
They then asked to feel my wings and if they could use my sewing machine.

Thought 51

That may have almost killed me, but it would have surely killed someone else. I no longer ask why me. Why not me?

Thought 7

Our parents were supposed to be our blanket of protection. We grieve the security we lost when they chose not to be.

Our parents were supposed to be our blanket of protection. We grieve the security we lost when they thought they could be or wanted to be but didn't have the capacity nor capability to be.

Off White

I've done the homework, so my heart is pure.
I still can't help but wonder how my heart would beat if it were even more pure.
Why nine times out of ten, it's family or
the friends of them?
Why is it usually family or the company they keep?
Why did they do it before I could even speak?
So they could turn my coat off white without regret and in peace.
I'm still a kid, but I'm older now.
Yet, they were still bold enough to put their hands and different things were they don't belong.
I wanted to tell but I had a feeling it would come out all wrong.
What's worse is, what if I tell and everyone knew all along?
I did it though.
I found the words to speak, and those words blamed me.
This is embarrassing.
Now somehow, I'm the one that has to say sorry.
They turned my shirt beige and no matter how many times I bleach it, it won't ever turn back white.
And they came back again that same night.

Thought 30

What if the reason you went through hell during your childhood was so your child or someone else's could experience a peaceful one? Maybe if that trauma hadn't happened, you wouldn't be as aware and equipped to go to war for those who can't defend themselves.

Thought 78

Your body is no less sacred or beautiful than before. Your value to this day, is as heavy as a wrecking ball yet as precious as a fine China set.

My Unlocked Door

It seems we all know a victim,
but nobody has seen the person that did the thing.
I used to be naïve.
But I'm not to blame for what anyone else has done.
Now I'm the un-fun, serious one because after one drink I'm done.
Honestly, I'd rather have none.
I'd rather be alert, so I can better spot a pervert.
So I can at least fight back.
So I can wear my RBF that they say I have, to appear mad.
Because my friend smiled politely as she said no to a man that wanted her number, and he took that as her wanting him back.
So maybe, if I turn my face mean it'll make him rethink.
That way I can focus and watch everyone's drink.
I left my front door unlocked.
I didn't know I was followed home.
He walked right in.
He walked in because of him.
I left my front door unlocked.
I didn't realize until I heard the door open and felt my heart drop.
It seems we all know a victim,
but nobody has seen the person that did the thing.
Yet so many of us scrubbed our skin until we started to bleed.

Grief Is A Five Letter Word

Who all took that boiling hot shower, in attempt to wash the shame off somehow?
You can't tell me they're not around, so many of us are called liars now.
What's the incentive to speak?
We go into shock and survival mode.
We accidentally wash away evidence because we didn't know.
These stories are the ones left untold.
So believe me, you've seen a person that did a thing.
And yes, they are still usually family, or the company that they bring.

Thought 80

Avoiding and ignoring vital conversations that need to be had because they make you uncomfortable, only keeps the tradition your elders passed down of sweeping things under the rug alive and well.

Thought 79

Pouring and pouring into others flower box while yours is withered is not going to fill the hole where that flower that has been beautifully plucked once was.

Bargaining

I'll do whatever, as long as I don't have to ever feel a pain that resembles the pain I'm in ever again. I know good and well that's a promise I can't keep. The only promise kept is to me. And that's the promise of burn out and defeat sweeping over me the same way it always does, when I overcompensate for love. When I overdo and then feel used. When I water seeds with love and out sprouts emotional and mental abuse.

I put my time, support, and love up for sale in exchange for the same in return. But I mark mines down low, lower, and lowest until it's a complete free for all. I overly share and care for people I am invisible to. They don't give a damn about me. The only reason they were here was to take but I'm giving, so who am I to blame? Ultimately, it's my fault for expecting me out of someone other than me. Now I'm even worse than before. Now my heart is even more sore.

Thought 74

Often times the ones who hurt you watch in the distance, in awe that you're still alive. Most will reappear disguised as good to gain access to you and finish the job right this time. Keep your distance, protect your progress, and forgive from afar. Forgiving does not allot them re-entry or a response. You are not bitter for deciding not to be around people and things that you had to forgive and heal from; you are protective of you.

Accomplice

I'm too exhausted today to yell and fight.
Yesterday I told you I've been fighting for my life.
I probably should've kept that to myself, right?
You watched me go sit by the ledge.
But you still push and pick at me.
I think you like hearing me beg.
I have no energy to lend, yet you grin wider and widest demanding again.
I'm too dehydrated to make you drink.
I have my own holes to patch, or would you rather me let my boat sink?
You assisted in my breakdown.
You gladly twisted the knife around.
My main artery, you just barely missed.
I slowed my breathing and focused on me, but I'll let you think you've got your wish.

Thought 94

One day you'll never talk to that exhausting, draining person again and life will feel lighter.

Overdose

Stop overplaying your part.
Because although you have a good heart,
they take from you in greed.
Now what was once favors and nice gestures have become the new normal in their self-centered life.
Say no, set boundaries, and put yourself first.
They'll begin to wonder why you're not *"just doing"* anymore.
Trying to guess what purpose you could possibly have besides tending to and helping them.
Once they feel the effects of you wearing off,
the text and calls will stop next.
They'll then dispose of you like a used needle once you begin to indulge in your own good energy.
Stamped as weird and deemed selfish, because you no longer let people take advantage of and overdose on a drug called *You*.

Thought 27

They'll call for a favor but when the favor jar is empty, you'll never hear from them again.
Don't stop having the big heart that you have. Just stop giving it to those who abuse it in greed.

Thought 52

Self-care is the cold drink of water you take while climbing this rocky mountain we call life. It's not selfish of you to refresh and hydrate yourself. It's a necessity for survival.

Send For Me

I see black smoke coming my way, I hoped this day never would come.
But of course, I'm here as promised, standing my ground, right in it with you.
I need you to focus, don't drift, and please don't quit.
You're only being attacked because your force will soon be too big.
From here there is only upward, smoke has no choice but to rise.
Don't give up right before you realize your strength can only be homemade during your darkest nights.
Mind over matter is engraved in my skin as a reminder that only our flesh can be weak.
Your spirit is more than equipped.
Make all those in doubt of your power nervous.
The enemy wants you to break under pressure, to react, not to ask for help and fight back.
They'll regret the day you had to send smoke that's colored black.
Let's move.

Thought 84

Be protective of you. Stand up for you.

The Middle Child

I was born the black sheep.
I am the puzzle piece that won't fit.
Invisible is an understatement.
Be proud of me, like you are of your first born.
Hold me through my storm.
I conquered, I overcame, I found a way.
Cheer me on the same.
Give me my claps and flowers at the end.
You keep closing your eyes and ears during the parts where I win.
I'm like a stranger, just passing by.
I don't come around, and you people wonder why.
Put on my shoes.
How long would you last if it were you?
How about you hug me how you do, with the youngest one.
Bask in my presence, as if I were your oldest son.

Thought 59

Stop oversharing. Everyone's intentions aren't pure. Some only want to hear what you have to say when you're suffering because their misery loves company. They welcome your words with open arms and ears to hear how you ache but fall silent and become unavailable when you start holding your head high again.

You'll know when you've overshared because you'll feel like you've just convicted yourself. After you speak, you'll immediately think: *Why the hell did I just say that?*

Handmade Wool Sweater

You so desperately want to take that deep breath and let it all out.
I know it, I know you do.
For someone to spot the pain you wear and its prickly, itchy, uncomfortableness.
The sorrow you've been wearing for so long that it has become too tight of a fit on you.
Now you can't even begin to take it off without help.
Look at you, my beloved friend.
You're so constricted.
Although true, don't you dare do it.
Without it, you'll be naked.
Be mindful of who you undress wounds with.
Not them.
Save it for someone safe, on another day.
Don't overshare because notice, they don't have a spare shirt for you to wear.
So what can they possibly do?
Tell them for what?
They can't help you, not even if they wanted to.

Thought 40

Be considerate. The people that are always getting asked for help are not obligated to help just because they seem to have it all together. They don't have it all together. Stop abusing their superpowers.

Renege

I did it again, I didn't keep my word.
I feel guilty more than I should allow.
But there's always a reason.
I have a valid excuse, hear me out.
Before I can even follow through, I feel used.
I impulsively over offer because I don't want people to feel like they have no help... you know, like I do.
This feeling isn't just my imagination though, in the past I have followed through.
After the first favor, but before it's time to do the next, they show me loud and proud that my kindness is being abused.
That's when I renege.
Then I brace myself for the eye rolls, crossed arms, and sighs because now I'm the bad guy.
This too is my fault; I knew better than that.
I allowed their expectations of me tending to their lives to grow sky high.
In that regard, I'll handle me when I get home.
As for them, I'll just have to let them go.
The people who never speak to me until the day before they need something are now mad.
Because I said never mind this time to helping solve problems that were never mine.

Thought 41

People pleasing will be our downfall if we allow it to be. We often over pour into others in hopes of receiving the same in return. Instead of hoping another person is capable of reciprocation, why not pour into ourselves what we've always yearned for? Don't try to "favor" anyone into loving or valuing you. The moment you don't pour favor after favor into them, they will feel like you're being weird, mean, and selfish when in reality, you're just not a genie anymore. Renege, moving forward, stop agreeing to everything. This could be a trauma response to abandonment, hyper independence and so much more.

Last Slice Of Pie

I only started with half a pie.
Why?
Well, because someone gave me what they had left, and it was only half a pie.
Then she died.
I gave away one slice to a guy.
I still have three left so I should be fine.
And I'll do it this time, because that's what friends do.
It's just that I wasn't expecting to have to give up two just to help you.
That leaves me with one and I guess that's fine, that's all I need to survive.
Later that night I died.
My father asked my roommate how and why.
She licked her fingers and began to cry.
She told my family someone stole my last slice of pie.

Thought 39

Don't think that the only way you can give is by giving money. Time, compassion, solicited opinions, emotional space, and non-monetary favors are all giving and helping as well. Don't be afraid to remind people of that. And remember not to let anyone drain you of any of these.

Thought 54

Realizing that dream job after college wasn't really a dream at all. Mourning the satisfaction we thought we'd gain. Scrambling, desperately reaching for a pen to rewrite what our dream job and life looks like; like a man on the moon grabbing for a breath of air.

I Quit That Job Last Thursday

You can only email so much before it turns into begging.
The manager smiled as we spoke, but her eyes screamed *so what*.
The office is hostile, all the employees are catty and mean.
To address the problem, they just buy donuts filled with jelly and cream.
And then they're toxic again and again and again.
It's like I can't win.
There's an invisible ceiling I can't prove or pin, point is I'm fighting a losing battle; so I quit.
I don't make enough for this.
I tried to join the HR department, believe me, they could really use it.
But it's nonexistent or some secret, and I get it, so I quit.
I've been robbed of my time, with false promises and lies.
I'm the only one here with experience and a degree and my worth still goes unseen.
You go to school and chase your dreams.
Just to reach the finish line and find it doesn't mean a thing, to some.
I know my worth, so I quit that job last Thursday without a notice.
I quit that job, and they probably won't even notice.
I quit that job Thursday to have a three-day weekend.

Because Monday I started my new job with my new HR position.

Thought 85

Maybe your version was the wrong one all along. Maybe all of your roadblocks were strategically placed so you wouldn't end up in the wrong place and take up the wrong space.

Clocked In

And I'm not allowed to wonder when I'll ever clock back out.
I don't remember ever applying, but here I am.
I don't mean to complain but I'm drained, and no sleep is my new norm.
Guilted into changing adult diapers in exchange for the ones changed when I was born.
No one's life should revolve around taking care of someone sick.
I can't believe I'm even writing this; I feel so selfish.
But I have kids and bills and my own problems that need fixed.
You would've thought we were playing tag the way everyone scattered, and I became it.
I'm only asked if I need a break after I mention how no one seems to wonder if I need a break, or if I'm even alright.
It's okay, I'll do it either way.
I have to stay clocked in today, tonight, and tomorrow night.
To clock out would mean someone I love has lost their life.

Thought 35

A delay in your day stopped you from being at the wrong place at the wrong time. This is fate trying to protect you. What you are calling a bad day because your day has been slowed down is actually a good one. If everything aligned and went exactly how you planned it, you may have run right into a worse day.

Thought 49

Damn you're strong. Good, bad, and sad you still show up every day and I'm proud.

Depression

I'm disappointed it's gotten this far. I feel like a bystander floating, watching myself from another person's point of view. To see myself getting sicker and sicker by the day is a scary feeling; a deadly one. The constant humming buzz in my ear is eternal, at least that's how it seems. I'm left trapped in the "insane asylum" that *I prefer* to call my mind. No single medication prescribed alone is capable of saving my life.

I swallowed a pill called prayer followed by a shot of writing to take the edge off. That wasn't enough. I've always been scared of the dark, and this stage of grief is undeniably the deepest, darkest stage. I caught myself tip toeing around who I think was me last night. I kept quiet in hopes not to provoke myself because this could quickly become the last page I ever write.

Thought 65

Laughter is my favorite flavor medicine. Laughing wholeheartedly, eyes closed, with my head back. Tears made from laughter always taste the best.

Diamond Ring

I made a promise to keep going, that's a promise I can't break with something so pretty looking up at me.
I did a thing.
So that no man or woman could say that they introduced me to the luxury of you.
I bought a ring, a diamond one.
As a token of admiration.
As a thank you to myself for never giving up.
For standing tall all the times I wanted so badly just to sit down.
I gifted myself diamonds, I see myself in them.
They dance and shine in the distance.
Up close, I can see their pretty imperfections.
I gifted myself diamonds, so no man or woman could say they were ready to love me forever; before I, myself do.
I only bought it once I knew I was telling myself the truth.
I've fell in mud more than a few times.
And I won't lie, each time I'd lie there longer than before.
But this time, my diamond ring caught my eye.
I saw that it still danced while it was dirty, that's all the motivation I think I'll ever need.
Now I dance when life gets ugly, I can't get outshined by a ring.

Thought 11

The pitter patter of paws coming closer and closer is the only reason I don't stay in bed on my days off.

Murci

My creamy, curly, little dog with your chocolate dipped mouth, tail and ears.
We met on my miscarriage date.
It was the fifth year.
I was at the gas station, a smiling lady held baby you up for me to see.
Ever since, it's been we.
Me and my Murci.
Traveling and making memories.
I'm not the best dog mom, but I'm trying so please have mercy on me.
I tend to quit things, but I made a promise not to quit you.
I will give you a colorful dog life if that's the only thing I ever do.
You will run, you will swim, and you will sight see.
You will taste all the flavors and textures right along with me.
You will have a beautiful story, the prettiest I've ever wrote.
You will only need one set of humans in this lifetime, I'll still be here when you get old.
And you'll feel the same arms around you, when the time comes to let go.

Thought 4

When I'm sad I look over at my dog standing in the doorway wagging his tail; innocently oblivious of how cruel the world is.

Paw Shaped Hole In My Heart

I still have your bed and bowls set up the way they've always been.
All of your toys are still in your play bin.
Your collar is waiting on you to wear it again.
I thought I heard the patter of your paws through the hall, but that was just the sound of my heart beating after all.
I pulled the cover over my head, that's usually the part where you jump onto the bed.
I thought I felt your tail wagging by my feet, but that was all merely a dream.
I thought I felt you lying on my chest, waiting for the thunderstorm to start.
But that was just the paw shaped hole you left in my heart.

Thought 32

No matter how small anyone's amount of time on earth was, their ultimate purpose has been served and the butterfly effect has begun.

Thought 91

Although my surroundings are crumbling, I have to keep going. God instructed me to write, to move. And I'm going to do just that.

Front Row At The Funeral

I lost the one person that kept me sane, I'll never be the same.
I'd give everything I own without a thought to spend one more day sitting, laughing, and talking how we used to.
You had uncrossed off plans for tomorrow that you never got to.
It hurts to feel happiness without you.
The milestones I dreamed of crossing off are just unmarked calendar days that pass, since they weren't celebrated with you.
I don't know why or what I'm doing anymore.
This is usually the part where I quit.
I haven't.
You'd be proud, and we would've started to laugh and smile by now for no particular reason.
I'm lost here, without my person.
How are you will never be as good, but I've been managing to make do with just being okay.
I pray I can say "good" again one day.
It still won't be as good as it could be if you were able to stay.
I never imagined your funeral would come before I finished writing what all I had to say.

Thought 31

Although death may appear unexpected, the death date was assigned right along with the birthday. Nothing can stop the sun from setting on that exact date.

Thought 83

Often the road to healing is a dark, long, and lonely one. Sometimes so dark you can't even see your hand in front of your face. Walk it anyway. Just remember, if you trip and fall, don't be scared to crawl.

Alone

I've become accustomed to reserving a table for one.
I cry real tears.
I laugh a true laugh.
I talk to myself out loud often.
I'm more of a listening ear than any friend has ever been.
I think I like it here, it's genuine.
It's safe here.
In fact, I might stay here, and permanently be alone.
If anyone comes looking for me, I'll just pretend I'm not home.

Thought 98

Isolation doubles as both medicine and poison. It's a necessity, yet an addictive drug. Fall in love with being in your own presence, but don't give up on finding the right people to do life with. At least give it a try. Take a break yes, but don't forget to come back.

Sticks & Stones

Sticks and stones can be thrown, but sometimes words get thrown harder.
They stick with me forever, even though each time I throw them farther.
They beat me down every day, and those hits turn into mental scars.
Words trigger my disorders; they add fuel to my mental disease.
The scars I got from words are much deeper than the scars on my skin will ever be.
Words are what bruised my thoughts and self-esteem.
Especially those spiteful words that broke loose and bit down hard one good time.
Words are strong, and they have stamina.
Words run ramped through my mind nonstop, hundreds, thousands, if not millions of times.
Your words replaced the words I thought of me.
In my brain, they cackle and sit front row.
The words that hurt are all I hear; they won't shut up, overtalking all the good words that I know.
I'm a prisoner, I've been kidnapped by these words, and they won't let me go.
They haunt me and keep me up at night.
Words kill, that makes them murderers, they've taken so many lives.

Words seep into the soul.
Words can rot and grow mold.
Or you can plant good words, that help heal and promote growth.

You Can Sit With Me

A bully usually has been bullied themselves.
Usually in their home, so that's all they've ever known.
Until they learn to unlearn and break the cycle, they will never be able to grow.
Unhealed hurt people hurt people, when and where they think they can.
The things they do and say has nothing to do with you.
Misery loves company.
So they project their thoughts of themselves onto you.
Whatever it takes to make you feel how they feel is exactly what they'll do.
Bullies are made of glass, fragile and I can see right through.
They're obsessed with ruining your day because they're dangerously obsessed with you.
It's the way you think.
It's how you carry yourself.
It's because you're brave enough to still walk past.
It's the love you get.
It's the things you have.
It's because no matter how hard they bully,
you still show up.
You are the art at the museum that says: *do not touch*.
That fine, rare piece that they desperately want to break just because.
Tell everyone around you and make it known.

It may seem like it but trust me, you're not alone.
Speak, on behalf of the timid and soft spoken I have yet to reach.
And if you have to repeat yourself until you reach the right ears, then let that be exactly what you do.
No matter what, don't you go silent.
Because that's exactly what a bully would want you to do.

Thought 62

This is the third winter I cut off all my hair. It's only an inch long. I did it while laughing and talking on the phone. Goes to show, you can't just guesstimate emotions by face or tone.

Seasonal Depression

I can feel me changing.
Disappearing again, I can see me fading.
I can feel the sad passing over the cracks in my mask.
I taste it seeping in.
A battle I train for every year, but never win.
We're not able to fake it, are we?
Not this year, self I'm so sorry.
When the leaves fall, I start ignoring phone calls.
Muting messages.
My phone is on silent, the sound is triggering.
Selfish ego makes them mad I don't reply.
Meanwhile, I'm trying hard tonight not to die.

Level 99

I sat criss crossed on the floor.
My eyes full, like a tall glass of water filled to the tippy top.
Processing, trying my hardest not to blink because for that glass of water to overflow, it only needs one bump or one last drop.
A silence so loud the walls could crack filled the room.
In the distance, I could hear the noise of the world carrying on.
I'm usually strong, but in this moment, I feel so weak.
Is this defeat?
I did everything I could think of and level 99, I just can't beat.
I tried, I beat the odds, I overcame.
I beat level after level of this sick and twisted game.
I even learned all the codes.
I mean, these are all the codes I've got, these are the only codes I know.
I've had countless early mornings and double that of late nights.
I've been hurt since level 1.
I haven't even got to stop to check my wounds.
And there's no manual, at least not one written for my eyes to use.
Still, I was doing it; each level I got through.
All the way to level 99, just to still lose.

Thought 53

Get up, stand up right now. We have work to do and a purpose to get to. We have to keep going, let's move.

Thought 45

Assumption is the thief of clarity. Never blindly assume.

Last Time Was The Last Time

I call, but I will never get another call.
No more unplanned random trips to the mall.
I miss you, although you're still standing here.
My heart aches, I counted thirteen medications you have to take.
The questions I have that I haven't asked will remain unanswered.
Like a letter that slipped between the racks at the post office.
Or a new number scribbled down on scrap paper and shoved through the hole in my jacket pocket.

Thought 60

Those faint gusts of wind that brush across your face and slide down your spine are those we miss coming to pay a visit.

Thought 19

Why would you quit in the midst of chaos? Is this where you want to reside?

Just Keep Writing

There's one thing I do know, it's that I'll always choose to write.
I will write to save my life.
I choose to stay and fight to write.
I'll choose to write every single time.
I may break down in tears and cry,
but I'll write standing up tonight.
I used my knee as a desk this time.
My pen loves me the most, I write.
And when it dries out, I'll just type.
And if I can't type, I'll just talk tonight.
Keep going, everything will be alright.
I am the author of my life, and I say a semicolon will suffice; so, let's write.
My book will not end here, I will write right here all night.

Thought 61

Do not allow your spirit to be broken. Collect memories, journals, and pictures of yourself to look back at. These are proof you were here, proof you lived your life, and proof you survived.

Their Only Ammo

You're beautifully contagious, you have so much that's good about you.
They could never reach the beauty you have within.
Their only option was trying to damage the surface of your skin.
They hoped you wouldn't feel as pretty if they took your looks away from you.
They didn't realize your pretty would still shine through.
That's because your pretty was made from deep inside of you.
They thought they'd break you down, but they only went skin deep.
The power and beauty you still carry is way deeper than their mind will ever be able to think.

Essentials

You are needed.*
Your energy, your outlook, just your presence.
What you have to offer this world can only be delivered by you and cannot be duplicated.
The space you take up is much needed.
You do it so imperfectly beautiful.
The weight of your existence helps slow this crazy world down to doable pace.
You belong in the empty space between fresh crops and air.
In the same row as clean water, shelter, and self-care.
Inside the most crucial, safe kept drawer labeled—
Essentials.

Thought 63

Gratefully savoring every good day like a bite of my favorite ice cream topped with streusel. Basking in this twenty-four hours and all of its deliciousness. I wish this bowl was bottomless so it would last forever.

Hug Me

The undeniable urge to hug a stranger because we both saw that, and at the same time, we both laughed.
The desire to hug the girl I crossed paths with because her outfit was cute, and after I told her, she yelled back "Yours too!"
If only I could let out a deep sigh and hug the guy in the car that stopped his lane of traffic so I could turn left.
The craving to lean my head on the shoulder
of the other coffee shop regular in the front of the line.
I've felt like this since we met.
She purposely didn't order our usual, because she noticed me pull in; and there was only one croissant left.
These sugary rain drops so happen to stop by in my life on my darkest days.
They had to be custom packed and sent straight to me, as a sign that everything will be okay.

Thought 46

I had writing for breakfast. I choose to feed my mind what it has always craved, my passion. With each word, my mind becomes satisfied, healed, and well balanced. You are what you eat, write.

Sock Shaped Tears

I am an artist.
My room doubles as my canvas.
This room is my safe place, it illustrates my unorganized mind and its growing pile of stress.
To pick up this mess is to initiate the work it takes to clear my mind physically.
I dry my eyes with a black sock to the thought of where to start cleaning mentally.
If I do one and not the other, wouldn't that make my life mismatch?
So, when I'm able to move forward in healing, my safe place will begin to reflect the same.
Progress could be made if I picked up a few things a night.
It's just, I can't right now, I'm paralyzed by my anxiety tonight.

Thought 86

If we pick up one crumb at a time on the days we can, we will eventually have enough crumbs to make an entire cookie. The smallest progress is still progress.

Saturday Afternoon

I may not have needed another blanket or flower vase.
Aimlessly strolling from store to store, like a stray cat going door to door.
Pointless to an outsider looking in.
Nonetheless, Saturdays that end with new items give me my dose of serotonin.
And, that purchase affords me one more dose of serotonin when I wake up in the morning.
Lost in my freshly adopted items I am, as soon as I reach my front door.
This is how my mother started to hoard.
I don't blame her, surrounded by bite size pieces of comfort.

Thought 97

You do have a choice. The other option may hurt or be harder, but the choice is still ultimately yours. Wake up every morning and choose to move. Remove whatever you have to remove so that you can continue your journey towards peace and happiness. Start choosing yourself and watch how your surroundings and body thank you.

Solo Car Ride

With a house full of people, get away for some time.
You deserve at least that to clear your mind, to unwind.
If you live alone and work has filled your day, take a pinch of it back, ultimately, it's your say.
If you have no car, and the day took a toll, lace up your shoes, breathe out, take a stroll.
Even with no way outside, you can still leave the worries and bad thoughts behind.
You can still take that ride, down a street called: *your mind*.

Thought 14

Birds chirping won't annoy you anymore, they'll remind you that it's a new day and another opportunity for progress.

Acceptance

The thing is things will never be the same. This is my new normal. But since when has life not changed? Life is ever evolving, and I know I can't force it to freeze in place. There are chapters of my life I need to get to, and I can't do that standing still. I am no longer holding my breath. I am no longer savoring pain. I am no longer freezing leftovers from wounds and trauma to heat up and serve later. I choose to defeat and release my pain. My pain and scars only have the power to hurt me and the ones I love, so what good are they to keep?

I'm looking forward to getting acquainted with the new me. I choose to embrace each stage. Although I don't like every single reality that comes along with my new normal, I'm owning it; It's mine. This is my new beginning. I never imagined it would start to look this soft and feel this pretty.

Thought 42

Acceptance trying to erase, cross out, un-wrinkle, and go over top of things with white out; then realizing you have to put the pen down and turn to a fresh, blank page to finish writing your story.

Thought 38

Peace is expensive, but it's worth paying the tab.

A Pretty Penny

Nobody speaks on the price we pay for peace.
I'll be amongst the first to say—
I had to pay an arm and a leg to protect myself.
It was one hell of a fine, to protect my mind.
You'll lose friends and family that were never really worth your time; the same ones you've always had around you.
The ones you never realized were helping hinder your growth.
The heart breaking charge off to miss out on milestones and family events, in honor of your healing journey and new set boundaries.
The bill of judgement for distancing yourself out of the newfound love you've built for you.
The staggering tab of mad and offended people who are only offended that you feel they have offended you.
They don't care that they were disturbing your peace; only that you're doing something about it.
The achy feeling that washes through your body all the way to your toe and fingertips.
Face to face with the cost of peace in silence, realizing that you have no choice but to walk away for your own health and peace of mind.
If I have to foot the bill to be less stressed, happy, healing and properly grieve, then check please.
Every penny I have, I will gladly leave.

Thought 71

No matter how uncomfortable the conversation is, do something or it will continue. Remove yourself or address it and set firm boundaries. You don't deserve to live in a state of uncomfortableness.

1,2,3 and 4

Life's a dance we'll never perfect.
A choreography designed to be so hard, you can barely keep up.
A never-ending tryout, to outperform and compete while trying not to get cut.
Constantly moving your feet.
A dance so hard, most will never be on beat.
A dance so cruel, friends and family are willing to make each other trip.
A dance so fast, you have no choice but to get immediately back up; even with a busted lip.
The dance will go on, so hold on because it will be over in a blink.
Choose your team wisely.
You're only as strong as the weakest mindset on your team thinks.
One, two, three and four.
To be rich within or mentally poor.
Five, six, seven, eight.
One percent dance and ninety-nine percent fate.
You better dance, dance before it's too late.

Swimming Lessons

Grief, like the ocean, has its days.
When the water is still.
Today I'm able to deal.
Today was a good day.
Then, here come the waves.
Waves of sad and mad that bang into me.
Waves so unforgiving I can barely see.
But I will not sink.
I refuse to stop moving my feet.
It's the ocean versus me.
Me versus my grief.
The only way to win, was to learn how to swim.
And I did, so let the healing begin.

Thought 57

I'd be waiting an eternity for someone to come and help me. Instead, I helped myself. You can stop waiting now, no one is going to come and get you. You have to learn how to save yourself.

From Me To Me

Forgive me, I come bearing a gift.
It was free, yet the value it carries is so high I consider it expensive.
Mercy, I promise to let up on you.
You've never been right here, right now, so how would you know what to do?
And you're doing your best.
You my dear, are remarkably impressive.
You're building from the ground up, by hand with no tools.
Forgive me for bashing, bullying and belittling you.
I uplift everyone else and still manage to tear down you.
I plant your biggest doubts.
I've been your biggest critic, and I keep you up at night.
I am mortified, I'm the last person I should have to fight.
From today forward, I promise to be the biggest fan to myself that I can be.
Sincerely with love, from me to me.

Thought 66

Peace is a drink served only once you've accepted that your plate has realities on it you hate; but you poured sauce on top of it and ate anyway.

Iris Meadow

I was planned but still unwanted.
Planted and forgotten.
But you're free to go, the rain will help me grow.
You can tear my petals off, one by one for fun.
Deny me shade and water, hoping I'll wilt from too much sun.
I was planted, no matter how much you wish I wasn't.
Back a few weeks and a few nights, by a gardener and his wife.
And by sunrise the gardener and his tart hand told me to go.
A tart hand that couldn't stand to see me grow.
A pair that envied my green stem when it sprouted strong and tall.
A pair that dared to snap my stem just to see my stigma fall.
So I'll go, but the wind already blew my seeds across the street.
They carry my raw, uncut story.
So when I go, I'll go heard and healed.
If you look to your right, you'll see thousands of me in that field.

Thought 75

Acceptance is realizing that your wrinkles are wisdom, your gray hair is strength, and your climbing age is a badge of honor. Look how far you've gone. Look how long you've stayed.

Fine Wine

The most valuable gift given will always be time.
These eyes, almond shaped and colored, follow a beautiful timeline.
My highlights came free of charge.
My hair is perfectly seasoned with pepper and salt.
My age is climbing high, but my self-esteem climbs higher, I made that myself.
I wouldn't want to be anyone one else.
Grateful for the growing number on the bottom of my page.
Honored to soak up what each passing year has to say.
This age is my new favorite age.
That is, until my next birthday.

Thought 43

Don't let pages like 3, 40, and 133 rob you of reading what's on page 188. Flip to that fragile page, admire its pain and shuffle back up to the page where you left off, keep moving towards healing.

Main Character

I'll spend the whole night out if I want to.
I'll wake up at two in the afternoon, if that's what I choose to do.
I'll agree to brunches and trips and cancel them later if I no longer want to go.
If they ask why, the reason will simply be: B*ecause I said no.*
Me changing my mind is valid enough of reason not to go.
I'll wait until my thirties to try and have kids.
And if I waited too long, well then who gives a shit.
I'll switch jobs and careers until it feels right.
I'm the main character in this show.
I'll do what I want, this is my life.
I'll wander around the world.
They denied my absence request last night.
I'll call off work while I'm on my way to my flight.
I'll stay single until I am loved.
And oh well if that means I never get to wear white.
I'll rip up the step-by-step plan I wrote for my life.
That plan isn't going to go exactly as planned anyway, and that's okay.
I'll be the misfit, the black sheep that lived my life.
And however it turns out, is exactly right.

Thought 13

A deep breath that feels like medicine instead of poison followed by an exhale of content. This is acceptance.

Let Them Go

Don't you dare beg, or over explain, or try to get them to see it from your point of view.
This is nothing new, I'm sure by now the bad traits outweigh the few good ones.
The bad parts repeat and reappear how rashes do, you know they do.
Let them go.
So you can cross the road.
Let them live in whatever reality they see fit for them and their life, and you go do the same.
Because life tastes a lot sweeter when you taste it from the comfort of your own lane.
Go grow and travel and experience things that were probably only meant for you.
Let them go, so you can fly a little further.
Let them go, because it hurts.
Yes, it'll hurt for them to leave, but if they stay it'll hurt worse.
The tingling sensation of them feels familiar to the touch, but it burns because those there are fire ants.
Let them go.
Because you're starting to sound like a broken record.
And for the record, they're keeping record of how many times you said what you wouldn't tolerate and then tolerated from them.

They don't take a word you say serious.
Stop waiting on them to leave, they won't.
Why would they?
You, let them go.
Because your intuition said so.
Let them live in whatever reality they see fit for them and their life, and you go do the same.

Thought 64

I could get used to this. The calm, warming feeling of acceptance melting my mind's worries away. At peace with what has come to pass and what hasn't arrived yet. My mind, body, and soul welcome the next chapter of life with open arms and a hug at the front door.

Thought 88

If you ever feel weak or like you can't function from missing me, know that I would want you to read thought 53.

I'm Happy For You

Look at you, smiling all wide.
I'm happy you're happy and that you mean it this time.
You deserve everything good under the sky.
I'll be cheering from over here.
I knew if you kept going everything left would eventually turn right.
I'm so happy you had the strength to fight.
I'm happy for your growth and that you had the stamina to write.
I'm happy you were able to write what you wrote.
And look, you've written out such a pretty book.
I love that you were able to title it: *My Life*.
I knew this day would come, the one where you'd be happy and at peace.
It's as mesmerizing as I always dreamed.
The day you sent a smoke signal and the smoke you sent was pink.

RBF

It's harder than it seems to cut out a shape different than your natural face.
You asked me to cut out a circle shape.
But my fingers naturally cut in the shape of a star.
Whatever you're thinking I'm thinking, I'm not, so don't think too hard.
You mean to tell me I have the power to sway you with one look?
You're so judgmental, why are you judging the cover of my book?
My head is high, face fierce and firm; deciding if I should add an aloe or a fern to my plant collection.
I walk strong and confident and to you my face might just be too much.
I'm minding my business, thinking of where to eat for brunch.
Without one word, you assume I'm mean.
Approaching and following me with rude remarks.
After I reply to your mean, you'll say— "See." And how you knew I'd be mean.
I don't have to explain a thing, but I do want to clarify what RBF means.
You've crossed paths with one of the most radiant, most beautiful, friendliest souls you never gave a chance to see past skin deep.

Thought 87

Friends are the ones we love without the condition of being related. We chose them, they are handpicked family members. Hold on to the authentic friends that make this bumpy road trip called life better. Make time for them, they are the seat belts we need.

Growing Pains

Our lives went two and three and four separate ways
like balls on a pool table do.
So did our outlooks and perspectives, rightfully so.
Because life looks different from everyone's own point of view.
And maybe, just maybe, no one is wrong but maybe we all are.
That part doesn't even matter.
We are gardeners first and foremost, then we are friends.
We are gardeners gardening, then we are family.
Tending to our own garden, keeping it as safe and upkept as we can.
Our droughts and dry seasons separate us into isolation.
While in survival mode, we built a high fence with a matching high guard as our lives bloomed.
Allowing us to finally enjoy the fruits of our labor in seclusion.
We paid in pain for growth.
This part is not about who outgrew who.
Our gardens just happen to be on two different streets.
So with no hard feelings, let's just release.
May our gardens grow so big that in another lifetime, the two might intertwine and meet.

Thought 6

Accept that you simply are not the center of everyone's world. That does not mean they wish bad for you or want you to fail. They have their own journey, battles and goals to get to. Just like you.

On a completely different note, squeezing into any space you're unwanted, intentionally unacknowledged, and intentionally not celebrated IS a disservice to your growth. Stretch out and take up so much space that you bust the windows of the greenhouse out. Outgrow everyone and everything that doesn't nourish your soul.

For Expanding Taste Palates Only

My surroundings are less than me, but they won't be for much longer.
I refuse to shrink myself to fit my big feet in those tiny, toy shoes.
I can't have the conversations I crave with the people I'm used to.
I crave to pour and be poured into a crystal-clear glass, and then swiveled around with intent.
I want my thoughts tasted and understood.
I want to curate naturally.
I yearn to stay in my element without having to word replace and water down my thoughts and goals just for them to be digested.
The conversations I crave are made for a sophisticated palate; a palate that I can exchange fine flavors and textures with.

I Like What I See

It's a crime for you to like you, for me to like me.
To genuinely like what I see.
To like how I look, to admire me, to like how I think.
To actually like what I do and like the food that I cook.
I like that I wrote enough words to make an entire book.
I like that the only opinion I care about is my own.
I like that I'm okay with being alone and that I don't have to always be on my phone.
We're expected not to believe in or bet on ourselves.
When you love on and nurture you, people tend to get quite.
They cringe at highly prioritized self-care.
I know it's rare to see and awkward to witness.
But the love I have for me, I learned and earned this.
I watered my tan brittle grass until it turned green.
I looked in the mirror and didn't look away until I could confidently say *I like what I see.*

Thought 20

You deserve to indulge in luxury taste, textures, and experiences in *this* lifetime. Not vicariously. Go do that thing you've always wanted to do.

Texture Tasting

The satisfaction I get from sampling the world is an indescribable one.
Memories of bliss intertwine with heart ache and hold hands because I never want this night to end.
They blend beautifully together forming a fine textured poncho.
If I could wear it forever, I would.
Memories don't stand the test of time without preservation; so I'll be jotting down the taste and texture of the night on the back of all the photos.

Thought 58

What's meant for you will have your name engraved in cursive print. It won't feel forced. You deserve a softer life. The best textures life has to offer will begin to unfold like silk once you believe with a sense of entitlement and confidence that you are truly deserving of it.

Vicuña

Worthy of a softer life, no, *thee* softest life that life has to offer.
Excuse me, because we naturally set a ceiling.
I deserve the best quality of life.
Not even the finest of fabrics and textures are off limit.
I'm not ashamed to say the wool my cloth was made from makes my skin raw; but I'll be damned if that's all I get.
I refuse to sleep in this just because it's the fabric my parents came with.
They can have it back; I'd rather run around naked.
Strong like the day, yet vulnerable like the night.
My skin will feel more.
The new cloth I have the honor of cutting from, will be worth the write.

Thought 73

I will unravel, undo, and resew myself stitch by stitch by hand if I have to. I will no longer use that fabric, I'm worth more than it.

Life Is Short

To wait is to gamble.
I'm not going to wait until I'm done to have fun.
What if I'm never done?
Discipline is not starving myself of experiences, it's balance.
It looks like crossing off goals and still treating myself
in between.
I'm not waiting to travel; I'm starting right now.
I won't be putting off hobbies until I find free time, I'll be
finding room for them right now.
The goals and accomplishments that are meant to be will
find me; mines are already written in stone.
Who knows, we may even bump into each other as I go
sightseeing down another road.
Maybe the only way I'll ever get there is by "accidentally"
going where I didn't plan to go.
I'll never go straight to work and keep my head down
all the way back home.

Thought 33

We've held on to what wasn't good for us merely because it's familiar for far too long. Why not turn the page? What if this next chapter is the best one yet? Yes, there were good parts but the weight of the bad is heavy enough to break the spine of this book. It's time.

30

Cheers, to the end of an era and the beginning of a better one.
I brought my dog and my name.
Everything else is in flames in the back yard.
Even from up the street I can still smell the ashes in the wind.
These here are growth tears because I used to never want my twenties to end.
Cheers, to the years I spent young and dumb.
Without them, I would've missed out on so much fun.
Bittersweet memories of being twenty something.
Traveling all alone.
Driving to the edge of the country and calling it home.
I'm packing my twenties up, they tried to kill me;
they could have killed me.

Thought 2

Grief is like watching a movie over and over again. It's having points where I laugh, get mad and sad in no particular order. Knowing the sad part is a scene away and there's no way to change what was already written for that film. Screaming at the screen for them to do that one simple thing differently.

It's revisiting the emotions that replay and repeat as the movie does the same. It's accepting the gravity and beauty of the masterpiece. I understand and accept that this was how the film was made. I get it, I really do. It's just a shame is all, that those words were the words... that had to be wrote.

Why

To show others proof they too can survive.
To share the lesson that I was handpicked and assigned.
Lessons, that may not even be mines.
I need anyone who will listen to hear me out.
I may have something in common with you.
I was used, in a beautifully, tragic way.
I accept that there was never another way.
No matter what "*if*" I chose to try, no other version of that sentence would have replaced that line.
I used to always ask why.
What did I do in this life to deserve to feel this grief?
Why me?
It's because I was trusted to be pricked and then plant that prickly seed.
I was trusted to grow along side of my grief.
May you gain shade and comfort while standing under my tree.
I used to always ask why.
Now I accept that what was written was supposed to be wrote.
The reason why was as beautiful as I had hoped.

Thought 99

What if I told you, there was no next level; no next street or turn? Level 99 is infinite, and it's called acceptance. This is the ultimate level because level 100 doesn't exist, we just assumed it did. In level 99, all things are possible and not even the sky is the limit. Live in the now. Accept every joy, sorrow, burn, and bliss for what it is. Let's make the best of it. Until we speak again.

Sincerely,

Your Friend.

I'm Short

I'm short, but that's okay, something happened today.
My mother's mother passed away, before I could finish writing all that I had to say.
I did my best; I'm allowed to rest.
I'll set my pen down, to pick myself up.
I'm short now, but later I can make it up.
I won't dwell.
I don't care if people judge.
My head is up.
My shoulders are back.
What I did write is still bold, permanent, velvety, and black.
I am short.
But I never imagined I'd get this far.
Facing grief face to face has been daunting, healing is hard.
I'm short but I'm also proud.
I'm proud of me.
99 thoughts and 84 poems of grief.
Excuse me, this poem makes 83.
I've reached 83 by digging deep inside of me.
I wrote until my hands started to bleed; for 84.
I'm one short.
I've made peace with being short, I'm short for good reasons.
So I'll go, with a goal in mind for next time.
I counted and then recounted with tears in my eyes.

I watched my pen roll until it hit the floor.
I'm Short is actually poem number 84.

Made in the USA
Columbia, SC
29 October 2024